The American West

Anne McEvoy

Copyright © 2009 Bailey Publishing Associates Ltd

Produced for Chelsea House by Bailey Publishing Associates Ltd, 11a Woodlands, Hove BN3 6TJ, England

Project Manager: Patience Coster
Text Designer: Jane Hawkins
Picture Research: Shelley Noronha
Artist: Deirdre Clancy Steer

Library of Congress Cataloging-in-Publication Data
McEvoy, Anne.
  The American West / Anne McEvoy.
    p. cm. -- (Costume source books)
  Includes bibliographical references and index.
  ISBN 978-1-60413-382-0
  1. Clothing and dress--West (U.S.)--History--Juvenile literature. 2. West (U.S.)--Social life and customs--Juvenile literature. I. Title. II. Series.

GT617.W47M33 2009
391.00978--dc22

2008047261

Printed and bound in Hong Kong

10 9 8 7 6 5 4 3 2 1

The publishers would like to thank the following for permission to reproduce their pictures: Art Archive: 5 (Global Book Publishing), 9 (Gift of Olin Corporation, Winchester Arms Collection/Buffalo Bill Historical Center, Cody, Wyoming), 12 (Gift of Mrs J. Maxwell Moran/Buffalo Bill Historical Center, Cody, Wyoming), 18 (Gift of Clara S. Peck/Buffalo Bill Historical Center, Cody, Wyoming), 24 (Adolf Spohr Collection, Gift of Larry Sheerin/Buffalo Bill Historical Center, Cody, Wyoming), 28 (Bill Manns), 52 *detail* (Bill Manns); Bailey Publishing Associates Ltd: *contents page*; Bridgeman Art Library: 10 and *detail* (Private Collection/Peter Newark American Pictures), 16 (Private Collection/Peter Newark American Pictures), 19 and *title page* (Private Collection/Peter Newark American Pictures), 30 and *detail* (Private Collection/Peter Newark American Pictures), 35 and 32 *detail* (Private Collection/Peter Newark American Pictures), 59 (Private Collection/ Peter Newark American Pictures); Saidos da Concha: 6 *detail*; Corbis: 7 (Bettmann), 21 (Patrick Bennett), 22, 25 (Brooklyn Museum), 26 (Kevin R. Morris), 27 (Warren Morgan), 29 (Marilyn Angel Wynn/Nativestock Pictures), 31 (Bettmann), 33 (Sunset Boulevard/Sygma), 36 *detail* (PoodlesRock), 37 (Douglas Kirkland), 40 (Lynn Goldsmith), 43 (John Springer Collection), 45 (Sunset Boulevard), 49 (Sunset Boulevard), 52 (Sunset Boulevard), 53 (Close, Murray/Corbis Sygma): Kobal Collection: 8 (20th Century Fox Television), 34 (RKO), 36 (CBS TV/MGM TV), 41 (Four Stars), 42 (Freulich, Roman), 44 *detail* (Europa/TF1/AJOZ), 51 (Warner Bros/ABC-TV), 56 (Paramount), 58 (Warner Bros/ABC-TV); Rex Features: 6, 14, 17, 44, 46, 48, 50, 54; Topfoto: 11 (Mark Godfrey/The Image Works), 13 (Michael J. Doolittle/The Image Works), 20 and 18 *detail* (Lisa Law/The Image Works), 32 (Topham Picturepoint), 38 (Arlene Collins/The Image Works), 55 (Topham Picturepoint).

Contents

Introduction

In 1781, America's western frontier was marked by the Appalachian Mountains. Forty years later, it had reached the Mississippi, but it wasn't until the 1840s that the first wave of settlers struck out into the real unknown—the "Wild West." This vast region included the grasslands of the Great Plains, semi-desert in the southwest, and the valleys and peaks of the Rocky Mountains.

The earliest pioneer families, establishing themselves in Missouri, Iowa, or Wisconsin, were soon out of reach of stores and supplies. They relied on homespun and home-dyed garments and animal skins for warmth. Gradually, the influence of Native American and Mexican cultures fused with the European immigrants' clothing styles. The cowboy was born.

The American West has proved endlessly fascinating to writers, painters, moviemakers, and weekend re-enactors. From a costume point of view, it's probably the first period for which we have good photographic evidence. In which case, how have movies frequently managed to get it so wrong?

The answer is partly that, despite that evidence, most painters and writers were working long after the era had ended and they were already romanticizing it. Showmen such as Buffalo Bill brought a lurid version of the West to Europe and left behind some strange misconceptions. These days, fancy dress shops are busy marketing versions of "western" clothing that no cowboy would recognize. These are often not only inaccurate but also insulting and demeaning, particularly to Native Americans and Mexicans. So the first rule is, steer clear of anything from those sources.

Below: Many artists portrayed the days of the great migration west as a romantic adventure into the unknown, but the reality was much tougher.

A HOME ON THE RANGE

"Oh, give me a home where the buffalo roam,
Where the deer and the antelope play,
Where seldom is heard a discouraging word
And the skies are not cloudy all day. . . .

The red man was pressed from this part of
*   the West,*
He's likely no more to return
To the banks of Red River where seldom if ever
Their flickering camp-fires burn. "

Brewster M. Higley, *Home on the Range*
(1873)

Frontiersmen and Explorers

LIFE AT THE FRONTIER

Several years before the mass migration of settlers began, some intrepid souls had begun to explore the area outside the eastern states. The term "frontiersmen" or "mountain men" embraces a number of characters. Some were professional fur trappers working for large companies such as the Hudson's Bay Company. Others, such as the legendary Kit Carson, did a little trapping and hunting while also acting as guides and explorers. Others were just loners who enjoyed a self-sufficient life on the edge of civilization, keeping one step ahead of the settlers. "Backwoodsmen" were sometimes outcasts from society or refugees from the law, who lived by trapping, fishing, growing a few subsistence crops, and brewing illicit whiskey, or "moonshine."

THE FUR TRAPPERS

The lucrative fur trade was one of the driving forces of exploration of the wilderness region as bands of trappers ventured farther and farther into the unknown in search of pelts. The main prey was beaver for the European hat trade, although fox, wolf, and bear were also hunted; silver fox was especially valuable for its use as muffs and wraps back east. Initially, trappers had obtained their furs from the Native Americans they

Above: In the movie *Mountain Men* (1980), many of the extras were genuine re-enactors, known as "Buckskinners," who supplied their own costumes.

encountered. Not especially valuing the pelts, the Native Americans happily bartered them for weapons and other goods. Soon, however, white men also started to trap animals.

FUSION CLOTHING

There are two basic outfits for mountain men. In many illustrations, they are shown wearing soft deerskin tunics and loose pants, decorated with long fringe at the shoulders, across the chest, and down the side seams of the pants. This was a fusion of white man's and Native American clothing. Footwear was also inspired by Native American attire. Instead of shoes, mountain men wore moccasins, which gave them a good foothold on rough ground and enabled them to walk silently when hunting. Buckskin clothing was comfortable (although it tended to stiffen and crack when wet) and durable. Buckskin was also easy to make or patch up or to obtain ready-made by trading with Native Americans. Once the clothing the men had brought with them wore out, many mountain men turned to buckskin.

STORE-BOUGHT

However, given a choice and access to a trading post, mountain men generally preferred the kind of fabric clothes they were used to. These were, of course, imported, or at least brought from the east: there was no time in the mountains for home spinning. Shirts were wide and loose, pulled on over the head and with little in the way of fastening. Usually made of cotton or flannel, they came in plain red, yellow, or blue or sometimes a small-patterned fabric. Checks during this period seem to have been rare. Pants were made of wool, sturdy cotton, or corduroy and were usually blue or gray. They were high-waisted and cut quite full in the body, either tapering to the ankle or "stovepipe" straight, kept up by suspenders rather than belts. The belt was reserved for a sheath knife, slung from a holster at the back, and perhaps a pistol.

WEATHERING THE WINTER

Winters in the mountains were bitter. In cold weather, a vest might go over the tunic, and almost every mountain man had a capote, a warm hooded coat made from wool blanket cloth, which he could wear all day and then wrap around himself to sleep. Wool mittens were a necessity to protect against frostbite. There is hardly any evidence of trappers wearing fur. Although this would have been the best way to keep warm, their catch was far too valuable to waste on themselves.

Below: Davy Crockett, one of America's first folk heroes, in a buckskin coat and leggings.

Below: Fess Parker as Daniel Boone, in the famous coonskin hat.

A somewhat more elegant alternative was the fringed leather hunting coat, thigh or knee length, tied at the front but usually worn open. A painting of Daniel Boone, one of the earliest frontiersman heroes, who was instrumental in mapping Kentucky, shows him looking rather formal in a buckskin coat and breeches.

HATS AND CAPS

Headgear was usually a more flexible form of the beaver hat, with a narrower brim and lower crown than the ones worn back east or in Europe. Some trappers wore flat fur hats, but these were made of poorer-quality fur such as skunk. They were often decorated with a feather stuck in the front. It's interesting that the racoon-skin caps with tails that came to be associated with that other frontiersman hero, Davy Crockett, are neither seen in contemporary illustrations nor mentioned in the many accounts of trapping expeditions. In spite of this, the spin-off merchandising campaign that accompanied the 1950s TV series starring Fess Parker as Davy Crockett sold millions of these "trademark" hats to children all over the world, totaling $300 million in sales during 1955—just over $2 billion in today's money.

THE POSSIBLES

Because few garments had pockets, mountain men carried a "possibles bag," which contained everything they might "possibly" need. Made of canvas or leather, this bag had a long strap so that it could be worn around the neck or over the shoulder and fastened with a flap. A powder horn and various sheath knives were either slung from the belt or attached to the strap of the bag. Some of today's buff-leather bags or hunting bags can be customized and distressed to suit.

GET THE LOOK

Frontier costume is quite easy to re-create since the original items were themselves simple in cut. A soft-collared or collarless "granddad" shirt and brushed cotton baggy work pants, both in a larger size than usual, will do for starters, but remember the suspenders. Fly fronts, not zippers, were in fashion by the 1830s,

Left: Hunting in winter often meant a warm blanket capote and snowshoes. These prevented the wearer from sinking into the snow by distributing his weight more evenly. Snowshoes were made of a hardwood frame laced across with rawhide. This hunter has rolled his pants to the knee to keep them dry.

A USEFUL SHIRT

"The hunting-shirt, which hung almost to the knees and had a cape over the shoulder, could not have been more practical. Its colour, if it was of jean or linsey [wool and cotton-linen mix], was usually tan or a red compounded of copperas [ferrous sulfate] and madder [a plant used for dyeing]. If of dressed deerskin, its colour was light brown. Its loose bosom, which could be lapped over half a foot and was held shut by a belt tied behind, was perfectly adjusted to the needs of a hunting trip or of a scouting expedition. In its fullness could be stowed a small bag of meal and a piece of jerk for the day, pieces of tow [cotton cloth] for wiping the rifle barrel, and other necessities."

J. E. Wright, *Pioneer Life in Western Pennsylvania*

but many men still wore fold-down styles, which would be harder to re-create. A long hunting coat will cover any modern details. A basic capote can be made from an army-surplus blanket: these come in gray and often have an authentic-looking black stripe. Shoes or boots should be flat and of dull leather, laced with hooks, not holes. True moccasins came in many styles, but a pair with the classic puckered top edge would serve most purposes and can be made from a simple pattern or a kit. Buckskin is available from specialist mail-order companies, but it would be expensive to make a whole outfit from it. Unfortunately, today's various synthetic "suede look" fabrics will not hang as well as the real thing, but they are a possible alternative. Failing all else, soft brushed denim is available in a buckskin color. However, cheap scrap pieces of real hide are good for making small items such as moccasins or pouches.

END OF AN ERA

Between 1820 and 1830, there were said to be over a thousand trappers roaming the Rockies. But in about 1830, the fashion changed. Silk hats became all the rage, and the market for fur began to dry up. By the 1840s, the era of the mountain man was over.

Travelers and Settlers

Above: A painting from 1867 shows an idealized view of a pioneer family and their log cabin home. The men are wearing typical hunting outfits, but the woman and children are a little too clean and neat.

WHAT'S IN A NAME?

British immigrants on their way out west may have been a little confused when it came to buying clothes. In England, "calico" is a plain unbleached cotton fabric, thinner than canvas but still fairly coarse. In America, this is called "muslin," while "calico" means any kind of small-patterned cotton. And what the English call "muslin," Americans call "cheesecloth." So it's important to know what to order!

FIRST SETTLERS

The clothing the European immigrants brought with them was in the style of their home country and so varied slightly from one region to another. Once it was worn out, however, many men followed the trappers in adopting buckskin clothing, although women rarely wore this. Moccasins often proved more practical than shoes or boots, whose soles wore out and couldn't be mended, but many, especially children, went barefoot around their homes. It wasn't unusual for a woman to walk barefoot to a neighbor's cabin, carrying shoes and stockings to put on there.

HOMESPUN

Once the homestead was established and women could grow and spin flax for linen or shear wool from their sheep, homespun fabrics took the place of skins. A favorite fabric was linsey-woolsey, which, as the name suggests, was a mixture of linen and wool: sturdy but not especially comfortable, it was also known as "wincey." Home dyeing from plant material tended to produce strong colors, such as red, green, yellow, or indigo blue. Subdued colors such as gray and fawn were difficult to achieve with plant dyes, although clothes did fade in the sun to less gaudy tones. Fabrics were almost always plain. Few women were expert enough at weaving to produce patterns, and block-printing was not yet common.

Men wore loose shirts, straight pants, and vests; women wore ankle-length dresses or a skirt and blouse, usually covered by an apron tied at the back. A bonnet or a straw hat gave protection from the sun in summer. Unlike the fur trappers, settlers happily took advantage of any animal they could kill and skin. Fur hats and vests were a welcome winter luxury.

CHILDREN

Throughout the West, and for much of the period, babies were kept in a long robe until they could crawl. This was then shortened as they began to walk. Like toddlers through the ages, boys and girls were dressed alike in a dress until the age of five, except that boys' outfits were plainer. Baby clothes were plain white or unbleached, and washing them usually meant boiling, which was quicker than scrubbing. Once out of dresses, children wore versions of their parents' clothes: there were few concessions to childhood here. Remember that clothes were handed down from older to younger children, so several members of a family might be wearing clothes a size too big or too small.

WAGONS HO!

The migration west began in earnest in 1843 when the first wagon trains set out for California or the valleys of Oregon. After the Civil War ended in 1865, the tide of settlers grew even greater. At that time, it took at least four months to cross the country from east to west, and since each family

Below: Re-enactors undertake a wagon train journey along the Oregon Trail. The long wagon in the background was known as a "prairie schooner" because it resembled a ship in full sail.

Right: In this painting, a scout in buckskins (left) brings news of conditions ahead to a family on the trail. The woman and child are wrapped in warm shawls against the chill of the evening.

PIONEER QUILTS

Very little pioneer clothing has survived intact to show us what pioneers wore because after it had been worn, patched, mended, and cut down for children's clothes, the remaining pieces were cut up and sewn into patchwork quilts. The quilts themselves, however, have survived and give us vital clues to fabrics and patterns. The names of the quilt patterns are themselves significant: "Log Cabin," "Broken Dishes," and "Indian Hatchet" echo frontier life, while "Jacob's Ladder" and "Star of Bethlehem" suggest the simple faith of their makers.

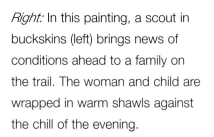

carried its entire belongings, plus supplies for the journey, in a single covered wagon, there wasn't much room for clothes. These had to be washed and mended along the way, and few people would have looked stylish—dusty and travel-stained is the order of the day for any character intended to be on the trail.

By 1857, half of the settlers going west were women, and the Homestead Act of 1862 offered free land to women and men equally. Once settled, women ran the home, churned milk for butter and cheese, tended crops, and made the family's clothes, but on the trail there was no time for weaving and spinning. Smart operators saw an opening for ready-made clothing, often made from imported calico, to be sold at trading posts along the way.

TRAIL WEAR

Women struggled in impractical long skirts, often hitching them up and rolling up their sleeves for work. There were two main styles of dress, both ankle length. One had full gathers falling from a yoke, a round flat collar, and buttons down to the yoke. The fullness of the fabric was gathered in by a belt at the waist. Sleeves were quite full, gathered a little onto the shoulder and into a cuff. The other style had a more fitted, seamed bodice, buttoning down the front to the waist, where it met a gathered skirt. The same look could be achieved with separates: a full skirt, gathered onto a waistband, and a high-necked blouse. Under both went a plain petticoat and knee-length drawers—not the ankle-length frilly pantaloons seen in movies. On top went a plain, waist-to-calf-length apron. Younger girls might wear a pinafore-style apron to cover their whole dress. Dresses were made of cotton or fine wool. Colors were blues, red or russet, dark green, or dusty pink, either plain or with small patterns of flowers, checks, or plaids.

Men wore a cotton or wool shirt, plain or with checks or plaid, sometimes with a flannel undershirt, and loose pants held up by suspenders. A bandana or scarf protected the back of the neck from the sun. This might be plain or have a pattern similar to that of the women's dress; silk was preferred but expensive. Most people tried to keep some kind of Sunday-best outfit to wear at the services (and funerals) held along the way. For men, this meant an unstructured wool jacket in black or brown, with narrow lapels, and a hat.

ACCESSORIES

The "prairie bonnet" was an essential. This was a gathered "mobcap," covering the hair and extending into a flap to cover the back of the neck, sewn onto a deep peak, which stood out around the face to offer shade. Streamers tied in a bow under the chin. Shawls came in two styles. The more practical was a large square folded into a triangle and wrapped around the body, while a more decorative version was rounded, sometimes edged with a ruffle or braid, and just covered the shoulders, tying loosely at the bust. Most women carried a drawstring purse or pouch, made from fabric similar to that of the dress. Sturdy footwear was

Below: These girls learning to sew on a re-enactment weekend are wearing typical calico print dresses and aprons. They're also wearing different styles of bonnet: the second and fourth from the left are wearing typical "prairie bonnets."

Right: The Little House on the Prairie, starring Michael Landon and Melissa Gilbert, ran for ten years on TV. Based on stories by Laura Ingalls Wilder that drew on her own childhood memories, it followed the adventures of the pioneering Ingalls family on the banks of Plum Creek, Minnesota, in the late 1800s. It's a good reference for costuming children.

essential since women often walked for miles alongside the wagon. Ankle-length work boots were more practical than shoes both for men and women, although children sometimes went barefoot. Hardly any men would be wearing heeled riding boots: few could afford a riding horse in addition to the horses that pulled the wagon.

A STYLE OF ITS OWN

This clothing is a world away from the fine imported fashions being worn back east in the same period. Even though it was made from imported cotton fabric, the cut of pioneer clothing was simple and functional: once the wagon trains had entered unknown territory, people saw little to inform them about the changes in fashion going on elsewhere. Even when

Wagon train woman and child

Prairie bonnet in flowered cotton

Hair swept up and covered by bonnet

No makeup

Scarf to keep the sun off the neck

Fitted bodice

Long hair tied with ribbon

Sleeves rolled up for work

High-necked dress with flat collar

Cotton apron

Overall pinafore

Gathered skirt

Cheap home-made doll in settler clothes

Knitted stockings

Flat shoes

Flat work boots

Above: Many of the pioneers out west were African American, like this family on their homestead in 1889.

TEXTILE CITY

In 1813, Francis Cabot Lowell set up a revolutionary textile production center at Waltham, Massachusetts, offering a complete service from raw cotton to printed fabric. He recruited immigrant workers but also many northern farm girls, who were attracted by the decent wages and independence. They lived in company boarding houses and worked a twelve-hour day, six days a week, but had the benefit of churches, schools, banks, and libraries. By the 1830s, the company had founded a whole new town, named Lowell, based entirely on the textile industry. In 1850, its forty mills employed more than 10,000 workers.

they had reached their destination and settled down, clothes were often cut from the pattern of an old dress unpicked and so remained well behind fashion.

WHERE THE CLOTH CAME FROM

Cotton had been grown in America, particularly in Georgia, since the mid-eighteenth century, but because it was a labor-intensive crop, the end product was expensive. Cloth was produced by small manufacturers employing workers weaving at home. They produced mainly simple checks and plaids, which explains the predominance of these patterns in home-produced textiles. Printed cottons were all imported from England or the British colonies. When the war of 1812 cut off these supplies, America was left dependent on its own production, and for a while this flourished. The Civil War, however, caused a setback by ruining the fields and freeing the essential slave laborers.

GETTING THE LOOK

Making pioneer outfits should present no problem since there are patterns available online and by mail order for classic dresses, bonnets, and shirts. Fabrics are also easily obtained in typical patterns. Anything in gingham, checks, or small sprigged flower patterns will do, although stripes are less common. Vintage clothing stores might still yield leftovers from the 1960s craze for prairie-style dresses, such as those made by Ralph Lauren and Laura Ashley: while they're not strictly authentic, they will pass or could be altered. Just remember, keep it simple, and avoid anything knitted, apart from shawls and socks. Although diarists record women knitting while their husband drove the wagon, sweaters were still things of the future. Don't forget that few pioneer men owned a six-gun or wore a gun belt, although they probably had a rifle inside the wagon.

CHOOSING A CHARACTER

The popular TV series *Wagon Train*, based on the 1950 John Ford film *Wagon Master*, ran from 1957 to 1965. Focusing on the core personalities necessary to the journey, along with various travelers whose adventures formed the weekly drama, it's a handy guide to some classic characters. The wagon master, in charge overall, rode on horseback ahead of the wagons. He'd be wearing a shirt and vest, brown pants, boots with spurs, and a gun. The scout, who rode ahead of the convoy, might be a Native American with local knowledge. Even if he was a white man, he could be wearing a fringed buckskin jacket. The cook would be wearing a long apron over his ordinary clothes (but not a chef's hat). A typical traveling family, including grandparents, would be dressed in the outfits described above, with children dressed like their parents. The family dog may well have accompanied them on their trek for protection and hunting. Remember, too, that after the Civil War, freed slaves often sought a new life in the West, although African-American settlers aren't often seen in movies or TV shows.

Right: The TV series *Wagon Train* had all the classic characters, (clockwise from top): trail boss, foreman, cook, apprentice, scout.

CHAPTER 3

Native Americans

HIAWATHA

" *From his lodge went Hiawatha,*
Dressed for travel, armed for
*   hunting;*
Dressed in deer-skin shirt and
*   leggings,*
Richly wrought with quills and
*   wampum;*
On his head his eagle-feathers,
Round his waist his belt of
*   wampum,*
In his hand his bow of ash-wood,
Strung with sinews of the reindeer;
In his quiver oaken arrows,
Tipped with jasper, winged with
*   feathers;*
With his mittens, Minjekahwun,
With his moccasins enchanted. "

Henry Wadsworth Longfellow,
The Song of Hiawatha,
Part IV: Hiawatha and
Mudjekeewis (1855)

COWBOYS AND INDIANS

The relationship between Native Americans and the white settlers was certainly an uneasy one but probably not as bad as represented by the early movies and even 1950s TV, which demonized Native Americans without making any real effort to investigate their culture. They were presented almost without exception as bloodthirsty opponents, attacking wagon trains and stagecoaches. In reality, this rarely happened, at least in the early days. However, as more and more settlers appeared, disturbing the buffalo herds and occupying land, the Native Americans were edged out of their hereditary territory.

Some movies have tried to redress the balance, notably Kevin Costner's *Dances With Wolves*, which presented the culture of the Lakota Sioux

Below: Three representations of Native Americans, from left to right: Osage, from Oklahoma; Iroquois, from what is now upstate New York; and Pawnee, from present-day Nebraska.

Right: Chief Sitting Bull of the Sioux, in full regalia, is seen here with Buffalo Bill in 1885, while on tour in their "Wild West" show. Sitting Bull's clothing thrilled audiences and set the style for the "Indian" costume.

with understanding and tact. When costuming Native Americans, try to do the same. However, it's not simple. Almost every aspect of life, from clothing and decorative imagery to housing, differed from one group of peoples to another, depending on where they lived. Obviously, this demands detailed research for accurate costuming. But for general purposes, it will do to know enough to avoid embarrassing mistakes, such as giving an Iroquois a long, feathered headdress when in fact these were only worn by Plains tribes. Many of these misconceptions originated with Buffalo Bill's traveling shows because audiences, enthralled by his Sioux "Indian braves," took them as representative of all Native Americans. Nevertheless, it's true that the Plains culture is the one with which we're most familiar.

But it's important to know at least which objects or styles of clothing came from which region. So who was where, and how did they live?

NORTH . . .

The abundant cedar forests that covered the northwest Pacific seaboard dictated the lifestyle of local tribes such as the Chinook and the Haida. They lived in wood cabins, traveled in hollowed-out log canoes, and developed a rich tradition of wood carving, including the famous totem poles. The complex figures carved into the poles represent characters from folk tales, celebrate significant local events, and record family lineage. One thing they were not was objects of worship, as Christian missionaries assumed. These tribes were famed for their "chilkat" blankets and capes, woven from goat hair and cedar bark, worn over a wraparound "skirt."

The northeast, on the other hand, was rich in birch trees, and so the Shawnee, the Huron, and the Five Nations of Iroquois used birch bark for their canoes and to make useful containers. They were farmers, and images of the corn, beans, and squash they grew appear in their crafts, especially the jewelry. They also collected shells from the sea- and lake-shore, which they traded as "wampum." The men wore a loincloth and

BUFFALO BILL

William Frederick Cody, otherwise known as "Buffalo Bill," was an adventurer who was engaged to kill buffalo on a massive scale in order to feed workers building the first railroad across America. He was known to have killed 4,280 in 18 months between 1867 and 1868. Cody is usually pictured wearing either a fringed buckskin jacket or a military-style tunic over close-fitting buckskin pants and thigh-high black leather boots. This outfit combines all the elements of his life as hunter, army scout, and explorer. It's also a showman's outfit: a romantic view of all his professions.

19

NAVAJO TEXTILES

Clothing blankets had been produced for centuries. However, when cheaper, commercially produced blankets became available, in about the mid-1800s, the Navajo made fewer wearing blankets and concentrated instead on making rugs in heavier weights. They kept the traditional geometric designs and colors, although in the early twentieth century, much brighter colors, from chemical dyes, crept in. Navajo rugs and wall hangings are particularly prized today and can be bought online or from Navajo trading organizations.

leggings and often went bare-chested in summer, wearing only a kind of sash across the chest. Capes and a kind of leather kilt were worn for ceremonial occasions.

. . . AND SOUTH

In the hot, dry southwest, tribes lived grouped together in villages of mud-brick houses, which is why they are called the Pueblo peoples. Settled communities, they farmed and grew vegetables, using the dye from their plants to color the homegrown cotton they wove into blankets and rugs. The Apaches lived in the same region but were nomadic. Clothing of this region was similar to that of the Plains tribes except that it tended to be made of cloth rather than skin. The Apaches were swift to adopt elements of Mexican clothing, wearing shirts and pants.

LORDS OF THE DESERT

The Navajos, who occupied land adjacent to the Pueblos, were expert weavers and produced fine textiles, which they traded with other tribes. They learned weaving skills from the Pueblos but instead of cotton, they

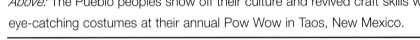

used the wool of sheep originally stolen from the Spanish. They also unraveled textiles acquired from Europeans—bright red *bayeta* wool was a favorite—and wove the yarn into their own pieces. They lived mostly in timber structures covered with packed earth.

Most of the "wearing blankets" you see are Navajo in origin, although they were much prized by other tribes, who obtained them through trading. They were worn like a cape: when the edges were pulled together, elements of the design met and completed an image. Each design was significant to the wearer. They were worn during the day for warmth and for sleeping in at night. Designs were mostly geometric: stripes, serrated lines, diamonds, and triangles. Black and whites, red, blue, and later orange and brown were favorite colors.

THE PLAINS

The tribes of the Great Plains included the Cheyenne, Cherokee, Crow, and Sioux. They were hunters who lived by following the herds of buffalo across the plains. Nomads, they lived in easily dismantled buffalo-skin tepees, which they dragged along on horse- or dog-drawn sleds when on the move. The buffalo, which provided food, clothing, and shelter, was the center of their lives and of their belief system.

A WELSH BLANKET

" I happened to enter the log hut of an old negro woman, being at the time in my mountain attire of buckskins, over which was thrown a Moqui or Navajo blanket, as it was wet weather. The old dame's attention was called to it by its varied and gaudy colors, and, examining it carefully for some time, she exclaimed, 'That's a Welsh blanket; I know it by the woof!' She had, she told me, in her youth lived for many years in . . . a Welsh settlement in Virginia, and had learned their method of working, which was the same as that displayed in my blanket. The blankets manufactured by the Navajos, Moquis, and the Pueblos are of excellent quality, and dyed in durable and bright colors: the warp is of cotton filled with wool, the texture close and impervious to rain. "

George F. Ruxton, *Adventures in Mexico and the Rocky Mountains* (1847)

The hides of deer, antelope, elk, and moose were all used to produce what we loosely call buckskin, but deer and elk were the most sought after. The method used by Native Americans to tan the hide was "brain tanning." This meant soaking it in a solution made from the brains of the animal, although other organs, such as the liver, spleen, and gall bladder, were also used, as were fish oils. This is sometimes called the chamois method, and it makes the hide both soft and waterproof. "Rawhide" is animal hide that has not been treated other than having the hair removed.

Right: These two-piece women's moccasins are of a traditional Apache design, featuring a beaded pattern. The turned-up toe prevented sharp objects such as cactus spikes and rocks from piercing the seam at the front.

CLOTHING

The nearest we can get to an all-purpose everyday outfit is the collarless buckskin tunic and leggings worn by the Plains tribes. The leggings consist of separate legs, each laced up the side and fringed, tied to a belt at the waist and worn with a breechcloth. This was just a long piece of cloth that went between the legs and hung down over the belt back and front. For special occasions, a breechcloth apron—painted or decorated with quillwork or beading—was worn over the leggings. Women wore a calf-length dress with three-quarter-length sleeves or sometimes a skirt and tunic, with or without a belt, and leggings. It was considered indecent for a woman to be seen without leggings. Both sexes wore a wool blanket, plain or patterned, over their clothes for warmth.

However, as interaction with white men increased, many Native Americans adopted elements of western dress. Striped drop-shoulder cotton shirts might be worn over buckskin leggings, and women also took to wearing cloth dresses in their traditional styles. Light-colored calicos were very popular, but also solid reds and blues.

FOOTWEAR

Deerskin moccasins were worn plain for every day or, for more formal occasions, decorated with beading or porcupine quills. Two-piece moccasins, reaching to the calf, were also widely worn, especially by

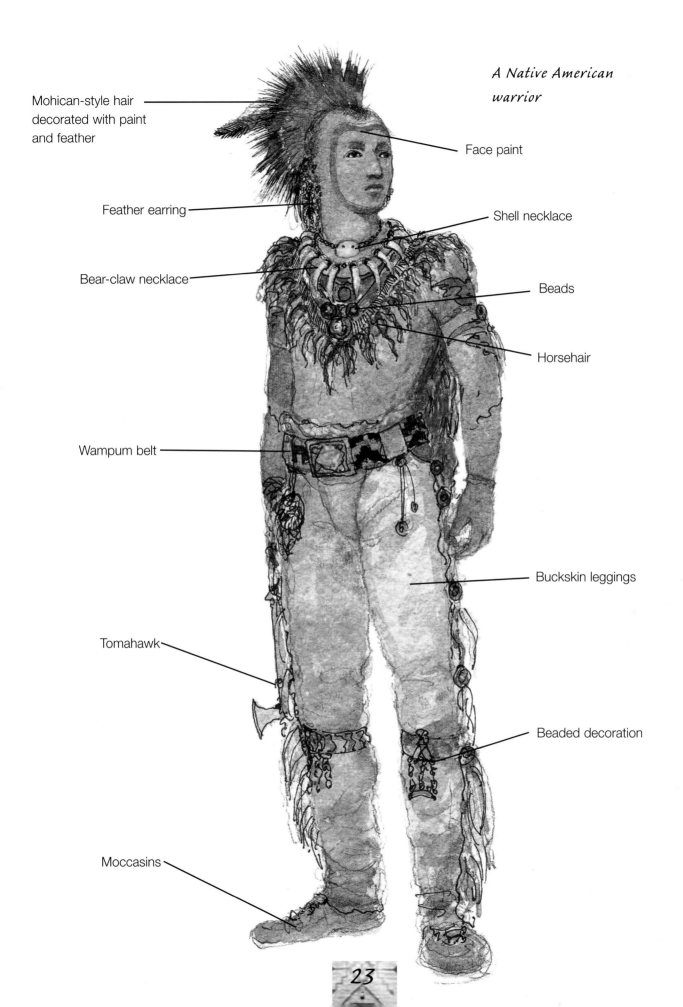

Mohican-style hair decorated with paint and feather

Face paint

Feather earring

Shell necklace

Bear-claw necklace

Beads

Horsehair

A Native American warrior

Wampum belt

Buckskin leggings

Tomahawk

Beaded decoration

Moccasins

women. These consisted of ordinary moccasins worn over leggings fastened under the foot, with the whole thing cross-laced with narrow hide straps. Most moccasins were soled with durable rawhide.

GETTING THE LOOK

The buckskin outfit is, of course, pretty much what the early frontiersmen appropriated, and the same comments about re-creation apply. There's no real substitute for buckskin. Patterns for these tunics and dresses are very simple since complex seaming hadn't yet been adopted: clothes were cut in one piece and sewn with buffalo sinew. For very basic productions, an oversized T-shirt, tea-dyed, will do, and a blanket can be easily customized with spray paint or dye. Re-enactors will also be relieved to know that breechcloths are seldom necessary for re-enactments today.

REGALIA

The feathered war bonnet, worn by Plains tribes, was highly significant. It represented a warrior's past achievements, one feather for each exploit, and it also protected its wearer in battle. War bonnets were made from the tail feathers of an eagle, the most powerful of all birds, and each feather was notched and decorated with wrapped thread to indicate how the honor had been won. The headdress had a band, often of beadwork, across the brow, and individual feathers, pom-poms, and strings dangled from the temples.

Similarly, the war shirt carried in its decoration memories of the wearer's past triumphs. The shirts were of deerskin with four panels of porcupine quill or beadwork

Left: This deerskin war shirt has panels of beading and quillwork across the chest and upper arms; attached to these are switches of what is probably horsehair.

decoration down the front and back and along the upper sleeves. Switches of horsehair might also be attached and symbols painted on. War shirts could be very colorful.

Oddly, one of the most recent movies to feature Native American costume was *Finding Neverland*, the story of J. M. Barrie and Peter Pan. All the costumes for the "Indian" sequences were researched and made by a company in . . . Scotland! They included a war bonnet for J. M. Barrie (played by Johnny Depp), a buckskin dress for Tiger Lily, leggings and war shirts, necklaces, and other accessories.

BUFFALO ROBES

These were not, as the name might suggest, fur robes (although skins were worn fur side in for warmth in winter) but ceremonial robes made from the skin of the buffalo with the hair removed. The softened skin was richly painted with symbols either distinctive to the owner or with particular significance within the tribe. The best buffalo robes were said to be those made by the Crow. An elementary buffalo robe can be created from thick cotton stained with tea and painted with symbols. It's important to remember that Native American culture was an oral one, with no written language. Images and symbols therefore had great significance.

DECORATION

Painting, bodily decoration, and the wearing of jewelry were never just decorative: they indicated age, rank, prowess in battle, marital status, and much more. It was possible to figure out virtually everything about a stranger by his or her appearance. The body and face were painted with paste that was ground with plant juices, bark, or berries. Color was applied first around the nose, using the middle and index fingers, then across the cheeks and

Above: Handsome Morning, a Dakota was painted by Harry C. Edwards in 1921. The woman pictured is wearing a fine example of a painted buffalo robe.

forehead. Men painted mainly lines on their cheeks, foreheads, and chin, while women applied dots to their faces. In both cases, the designs were quite simple: color was the main thing. Red and black were worn when preparing for war: red was associated with violent action, black with energy and life force. White signified peace. Green painted under the eyes was thought to give the wearer the power to see in the dark. Yellow was the color of death and was worn only when people were in mourning. Children's face paints can supply all the necessary colors, but it is important to keep the lines simple.

Masks were made mainly by the tribes of the northwest coast. They were worn for medicinal and ceremonial purposes and usually depicted animals. People believed that when they wore an animal mask, the spirit of that animal entered into them and they were able to share its powers. The same applied to the buffalo-horn caps worn by other tribes. Masks are good for children to make, using papier-mâché.

Below: This warrior is wearing a wolf mask in the hope of acquiring the animal's qualities of courage and cunning.

Above: A modern-day Native American in tribal dress explains the significance of feathers to his daughter. As a child, she wears only a single plain feather.

HAIRSTYLES

Men of the Plains tribes wore their hair long with a center part. Their hair could be shoulder length, with a headband of some kind—a twisted cloth, the favorite of the Apache, or a single strip tied at the back—or up to waist-length, braided or tied with cloth. A single feather or several bunched together and bound with braid or horsehair was tied into the hair at the back. Other tribes shaved their heads, leaving a single patch at the back, which was sometimes dyed. And everyone is familiar with the central fan of the Mohican style.

JEWELRY

Jewelry was worn by both sexes. Earrings could be of porcupine quills, a single feather, or metal disks but were always quite large and dangled low on the shoulder. The squash blossom design was used frequently on necklaces, as were bear-claw designs. Wampum beads were made from

STYLE TIP

If you want a Mohican style without shaving your head, make two parts and comb down the hair on each side, leaving a 2-inch-(5-cm)-wide strip of hair in the center. Using rubber bands to secure this panel, smooth the sides back with gel, then comb gel and hair spray through the center panel to make it stand up in spikes. Another way is to use egg white, whipped up like meringue, combed through the hair, and blow-dried.

shells found on the northern shores. Fashioned into cylindrical beads, they were woven into belts that were not only decorative but recorded information in their design, such as dates and tribal finances. Wampum beads were so highly prized that they were adopted as a unit of currency.

The most common form of decoration was done with flattened porcupine quills. It didn't need many tools: quills could be softened with saliva by just holding them in the mouth and then flattened with a stone and sewn into panels of deerskin. It's an easy technique to learn, and packs of quills are available by mail order, but be careful—they're very sharp. A popular item was the panel of diagonal quills worn hanging down on the chest. Porcupine quills and wampum beads remained popular even after the introduction of European glass beads in mid-century, although these were very much sought after. Oddly, rings were seldom worn, although silver rings set with turquoise stones are typical of the work produced by later Navajo craftsmen.

ACCESSORIES

Complete your outfit with medicine bags and satchels decorated with beading, quillwork, and fringe. These were worn across the body and contained objects believed to have healing powers such as bones or

Left: These gauntlets of fringed hide are decorated on the back and cuff with beadwork.

herbs. Women had various pouches for carrying mirrors, knives, or tobacco: these might be beaded or simple drawstring pouches of buckskin, which can easily be made from scrap pieces of hide.

WEAPONS

These varied from tribe to tribe but generally included a bow and arrows, spears, round shields, and the tomahawk, a kind of ax that could be used as a throwing weapon as well as in hand-to-hand combat. Some tomahawks had a hollow shaft, so they could also be used as a tobacco pipe: these were known as "pipe hawks." All these weapons could be decorated with painted images, feathers, horsehair, and bones.

Finally, if you're going to an event on horseback, remember that the pinto pony—black and white or brown and white—was the favorite steed of the Plains tribes. Most Native Americans rode bareback or with just a blanket, but some used Spanish-style saddles. It all depends on how brave you are feeling.

Below: These Shoshone warriors are holding coup sticks. Getting close enough to an enemy to touch him with the coup stick earned a warrior great honor. Note that the horses are wearing war paint and that, while the man on the right has a saddle blanket, his companion is riding bareback.

The Iron Horse

RAILROADERS

Many different characters helped open up the West. The first east–west railroad began operation in 1869. It cut down a four- or five-month cross-country journey to just ten days. The railroad took seven years to build, with two companies starting from opposite sides of the country and meeting in the middle.

The Union Pacific, going west from Omaha, employed mostly Irish immigrants and ex-soldiers from both the Union and Confederate armies. The workforce of the Central Pacific Railroad, going east from California, was almost entirely Chinese, drawn from the restaurants and laundries of California and augmented by thousands of new immigrants from China. Americans were fascinated by these exotic strangers, whom they christened "Celestials." They wore traditional Chinese clothing: blue tunics and baggy pants, along with conical hats. The Irish, on the other hand, wore ordinary pioneer work clothes—almost certainly the newly marketed Levi's jeans—while some of the ex-soldiers might have

Above: The coming of the railroad was a great event. Here townsfolk, workers, and—somewhat unlikely—a chief in his war bonnet have all turned out to see the sight.

Right: Panning for gold was a hard task. Many men owned little more than the clothes on their backs.

been wearing remnants of their blue or gray uniform, such as a Confederate cap.

The labor force included dozens of other subsidiary trades such as cooks, blacksmiths, and carpenters, all wearing clothing appropriate to their work, as well as professional engineers and surveyors, who would have been better dressed, in jackets and wool pants.

THE GOLD RUSH

When gold was found in California in 1848, thousands rushed from all over the world to stake a claim and make their fortune. They were a ragtag of nationalities and so might have been wearing almost any sort of clothes. A typical "forty-niner," however, would be wearing work pants, a plain or checked cotton shirt, a bandana for wiping sweat, a black felt hat, and flat work boots. All of these would be faded, patched, and stained. Living in a tent or a shantytown with nowhere to wash, he'd also be dirty and unkempt, with straggly hair and beard. Short hair was, in fact, regarded with suspicion since it suggested you'd been shorn as a treatment for lice. The tools of the forty-niner's trade were a pickax, a spade, and a round metal pan used for washing gold out of stream water. He'd also be carrying a leather water bottle and, in anticipation of good fortune, a bag for his gold.

RIVERBOATS

From the 1830s to the 1880s, paddle steamers cruised the Mississippi River between St. Louis and New Orleans, carrying freight and passengers. It was a glamorous if slow way to travel, and passengers were on the whole well off and elegantly dressed in city clothes. The 1950s TV series *Riverboat* (1959–61), featuring a young Burt Reynolds as engineer of the *Enterprise*, moved convincingly between the oily engine room and the public staterooms. However, the series was later criticized for not including any of the Africans or Native Americans who in reality had formed the majority of the workforce on the river.

STYLE TIP

It was considered unacceptable to appear in mixed company wearing only your undershirt. Many miners worked in just their flannel Henley-style undershirts, but heading into town or stepping into a saloon without a proper shirt over it was frowned on, even in those lawless places. And one-piece "long johns" were not worn until at least 1909.

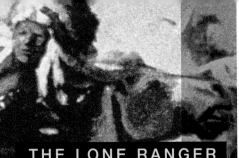

CHAPTER 5

Soldiers and Heroes

THE LONE RANGER

His adventures formed one of the earliest TV series (1949–57) after nearly 3,000 radio episodes in the 1930s and 1940s. Sole survivor of an ambush in which his fellow Rangers were murdered, the nameless and masked rider became a Robin Hood figure, roaming the West and meting out rough justice, accompanied by "his faithful Indian companion, Tonto," and his white stallion Silver ("Hi-yo Silver, away!"). At least Tonto—played by Canadian Mohawk actor Jay Silverheels—could claim that his fringed buckskin outfit was fairly authentic. But Clayton Moore, as the Ranger, rode the plains in a dashing but strangely figure-hugging shirt-and-pants outfit that never got dirty. His black leather gloves were not authentic either!

Above: The movie *Texas Rangers* featured a group of Rangers re-formed after the Civil War. Although the men aren't wearing uniforms anymore, they have made some effort to look alike, as ex-army men might have done.

THE TEXAS RANGERS

Formally constituted in 1835, the Texas Rangers were a kind of state militia, somewhere between an army and a police force. Initially they were informal groups of armed men who "ranged" around their local area, protecting settlers from Native American attacks and other dangers. The Rangers were active in the Texans' struggle for independence from Mexico, continued to fight skirmishes with Native Americans, and later became traveling detectives—hunting down outlaws and train robbers. The romantic image these exploits gave them was hotly promoted by newspapers and dime novels, making the Texas Ranger one of the iconic figures of the old West.

Despite their semi-military status, the Rangers had no specific uniform. In fact, they had to provide their own clothing, which might explain why they often looked somewhat patched and worn. Texan clothing was heavily influenced by Mexican clothing, borrowing in particular from the style of the *vaqueros*. The Rangers wore sombrero-style hats rather than the cowboy hat worn elsewhere and knee boots with a Spanish-style high heel. Gun holsters were worn high on the hip rather than slung lower on the thigh as cowboys wore them. They would also have used a Mexican saddle. Another Rangers' claim to fame is that they were the first company to use the new Colt .44 revolver.

THE ALAMO

In March 1836, a ragtag army of fewer than 200 men defended the old mission at San Antonio for thirteen days against the vastly superior forces of Mexican general, Santa Ana. Although all the defendants died, the siege delayed the Mexican advance long enough for General Sam Houston to gather the forces that eventually won Texan independence.

The classic version of the Alamo story is a 1960 film directed by and starring John Wayne as Davy Crockett, with Richard Widmark as Jim Bowie and Laurence Harvey as William Travis. Crockett and Bowie wore buckskin, while Colonel Travis, as a commissioned officer, wore an army uniform. The 1994 remake, with Billy Bob Thornton as Crockett, changed the costumes slightly and gave the characters a less romantic

Left: The three famous figures from the 1960 movie *The Alamo*, (standing, left to right): the well-turned out Colonel Travis, Davy Crockett (without the famous hat) and Jim Bowie in buckskins.

aura. "Remember the Alamo" weekend re-enactments take place in San Antonio every year, and, from the evidence, it looks as though most people prefer to echo Wayne's version of the costume.

THE U.S. CAVALRY

The typical cavalry uniform was a dark blue wool tunic, buttoned down the front with brass buttons and yellow epaulettes and rank stripes. It was paired with light blue pants with a yellow stripe down the seam, either worn with brogans or tucked into black leather boots. Finishing touches were a yellow bandana and either a kepi-style forage cap or a broad-brimmed hat with a yellow braid trim tied in front with tassels. There was also a black poncho-style cape for wet weather. However, uniforms changed over time, and there were local variations and different dress uniforms. Out on campaign, too, troopers sometimes wore buckskin jackets. When costuming a specific unit, check the details carefully.

Members of the U.S. Cavalry were armed with a saber and a revolver hung from a leather belt that went around the waist and across the chest and a rifle slung from the saddle. Re-enactors will need a broad leather belt with a buckle (nothing shiny) to carry the holster and a small pouch (for example, a coin purse). As mentioned before, the question of replica weapons is a complex one and should be carefully researched.

Right: Smart cavalry uniforms abound in the movie classic *She Wore a Yellow Ribbon*, but the buckskin jacket worn by aging captain, John Wayne, singles him out from the crowd. Second of John Ford's cavalry trilogy, *She Wore a Yellow Ribbon* was the most expensive western movie of its time (1949).

Right: In this painting of the Battle of Little Bighorn, 1876, the artist shows General Custer in a typically defiant pose.

HERO OR GLORY HUNTER?

General George Armstrong Custer was perhaps the U.S. Army's best-known character. His famous "last stand" at Little Bighorn, against a coalition of Native American tribes led by Crazy Horse and Sitting Bull, is another of America's "great moments," commemorated in a re-enactment every year near Hardin, Montana. Custer was a flamboyant personality who courted media attention and cultivated his own image. He invented a uniform for himself that included tight olive corduroy pants, a tight black velvet hussar jacket with silver piping, a sailor shirt with silver stars on the collar, and a red cravat. In his campaigns against the Native Americans, he wore buckskins along with his trademark red cravat. He wore his wavy hair long and doused in hair oil. Not surprisingly, this heroic but flawed character has been played by many movie stars, from Ronald Reagan (1940) and Errol Flynn (1941) to Robert Shaw (1967). Anyone dressing up as Custer today had better have the personality to match!

A NOTE ON FOOTWEAR

Boots were essential items for cavalrymen, cowboys, and anyone else who spent time in the saddle as well as on foot. Civilian "stovepipe" boots had a low flat heel and were cut straight across the top: those cut to calf length were worn under the pants; longer versions were usually worn with the pants tucked in. Military boots had a higher "Cuban" heel, and the top was cut slightly higher at the front than at the back. On average, they were about 14 inches (36 cm) tall. These would have been worn by cavalry troopers and soldiers in the Civil War but also by gold miners, cowboys, and cattlemen throughout the whole period. Most boots had loops at the top to pull them on.

STYLE TIP

Today's shaped riding boots are not right for the period, but there are many "rough-side out" leather boots available. Brogans were sturdy shoes that reached up to the ankle and laced up the front—very similar to Doc Martens or combat boots, either of which could be used today. Black brogans were regulation issue for the cavalry, although civilians wore them in black or brown.

CHAPTER 6

Cowboys

TRAVEL-STAINED CLOTHES

The typical cowboy outfit worn in movies is reasonably accurate if compared with photographs of the period—except that celluloid cowboys are usually clean and neat. In reality, long days and hundreds of miles in the saddle with few facilities along the way would have meant they were almost always dusty, sweaty, and travel-stained. Clothing had to be durable and functional. No frilled shirts on the trail!

After the Civil War, many Southerners returned home to find themselves out of a job, their land ruined and cattle roaming wild. The major market for beef was in the North, which meant that cattle had to be rounded up in Texas each spring and driven north, on the hoof, to a railhead. The big

Above: The 1950s TV series *Rawhide* portrayed the hardships and thrills of the cattle drive and launched the career of Clint Eastwood (center). The chaps worn over the pants were protection against cactus and sage brush.

cattle drives began in the late 1860s, moving first along the Chisholm Trail to Abilene, Texas, and then, as the frontier moved west, along the Santa Fe Trail to Dodge City, Kansas. These railroad towns sprang up almost overnight and became lively, not to say lawless, social centers.

ON THE TRAIL

A typical cattle drive was made up of the trail boss; the scout (sometimes a Native American); the cook, who was in charge of the chuck wagon; the wrangler, who looked after the spare horses; and any number of cowboys. Contrary to the images promoted by movies and TV, which show cowboys as exclusively white, many were Mexican or African American. Generally speaking, since most cowboys were Southerners, their clothing was heavily influenced by that of their Mexican counterparts, the *vaqueros*.

SHIRTS AND PANTS

An average cowboy wore canvas straight-leg pants; not all were Levi's, but these were popular and are certainly acceptable today in most costuming, although for true authenticity, remember that belt loops were not common until the 1890s. Over the pants, attached to a belt at the waist, went chaps of leather or fur to protect legs and pants from brush and cattle horns. These are quite easy to make since they don't have much shape and need not fit closely. Boots with high heels and spurs were essential, and those of Spanish tooled leather were particularly prized. Again, these are easy enough to obtain today.

Below: Butch Cassidy and the Sundance Kid (1969) portrayed the last days of the outlaw in the early 1900s, which is why the costumes are somewhat familiar to us. Derby hats were very popular at the time.

Shirts came in a surprising variety of styles and fabrics, which is helpful if you need to vary your characters. Some were collarless and buttoned down the front or only halfway; others could be laced up from chest to collar with fine leather braid. Some had bib fronts like a fireman's shirt; these usually came in red or blue. What's now known as "classic western style," with a yoke edged with piping, is a later variation popularized by re-enactors and was not common at the time. Shirts had either a conventional rounded shoulder seam

Right: The boots, chaps and spurs worn by this present-day New Jersey cowboy are unusual but based on authentic western wear.

or, more likely, a drop shoulder. These were the most common, since they were cut from rectangular pieces and were simple to make. In either case, shirts were loose-fitting to allow for maximum movement. For everyday work wear, plain colors seem to have been the most popular, but there were checks, too. Although cloth was still imported, the American cotton industry was getting into its stride again. Buckskin shirts and jackets were still being worn. Under the shirt went a plain Henley-style undershirt of flannel or fine wool and over it a leather or canvas vest.

ACCESSORIES

A bandana was essential, worn around the neck as protection from the sun or pulled up over the nose and mouth to keep out dust. These were plain or patterned, often with a paisley design. The cowboy also had a

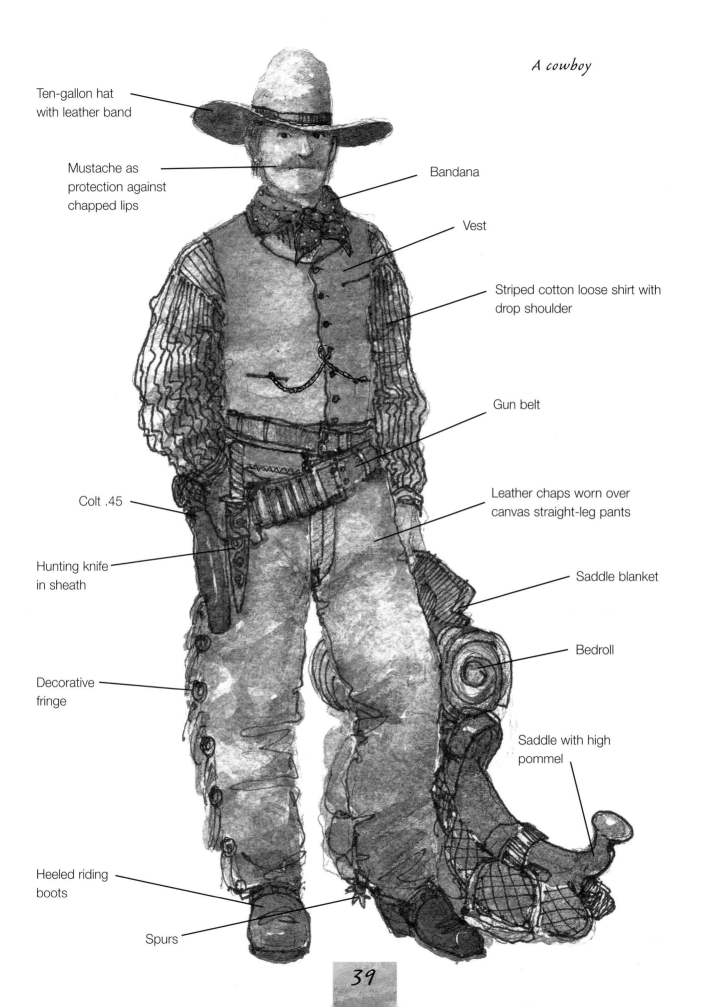

Ten-gallon hat
with leather band

Mustache as
protection against
chapped lips

Bandana

Vest

Striped cotton loose shirt with
drop shoulder

Gun belt

Colt .45

Leather chaps worn over
canvas straight-leg pants

Hunting knife
in sheath

Saddle blanket

Decorative
fringe

Bedroll

Saddle with high
pommel

Heeled riding
boots

Spurs

STETSON

John B. Stetson was a Philadelphia hatter who went west for his health. He invented the famous broad-brimmed hat in 1865, and it was immediately adopted by cattlemen and cowboys all over the country. He called it the "Boss of the Plains." With its 4-inch (10-cm) brim and 4-inch crown with a long indent in it, it's probably the world's most recognizable hat. Stetsons come in black, brown, gray, and light beige—hardly ever the white worn by "good guys" in the movies. Ladies' versions are also available in red and other bright colors, but they're hardly authentic.

waterproof poncho-style slicker for wet weather, which was kept rolled up on his saddle. Most cowboys wore a gun belt with a Colt .45 revolver, maybe a rifle slung across the saddle, and a sheath knife of some kind—the bowie knife remained the knife of choice for decades. However, as with the military, the whole business of replica weapons is complex and needs careful research. Every cowboy would also have had a rope lasso and a braided leather bullwhip coiled on his saddle for keeping the longhorns in line.

HAT SENSE

The cowboy's hat varied a lot depending on period and location. It's not true that everybody wore a Stetson, and a "ten-gallon" hat certainly didn't hold that much water (more like a gallon). It used to be possible to tell where a cowboy came from by the shape of his hat, the dents in the crown, the angle at which he wore it, and so on. Where the Mexican influence was still strong, sombrero-style hats with round crowns, made of soft felt, were mostly worn. The "Montana peak" had a deep crease down the front of the crown to channel off rain; the "open crown" had no dent in the crown; while the "southwest peak" had several small dents, like a Mountie hat. However, they were all made from rabbit or beaver fur, and all had a broad brim, which could be bent into different shapes. Hatbands, originally intended to tighten the hat to a good fit, were also

Below: The 1990s TV series *The Young Riders* featured a group of Pony Express riders in Kansas. Here we have a variety of clothing styles: fringed buckskin, the fireman shirt, cavalry-style boots, and various shapes of hat.

decorative, made of braided horsehair or colored wool, ribbon, leather, or sometimes Indian beads. Apart from the obvious advantages of shade and keeping off rain, hats were useful for carrying water, fanning campfires, and turning a stampeding steer. There's no substitute for an authentic hat, and no costume is complete without it.

SATURDAY NIGHT FEVER

Oddly, many cowboys were dandies while off duty. At the end of the drive, they put on their best outfit for a night drinking in a saloon. This was the nearest they got to fashion. Clothes included a high-buttoned, unstructured wool jacket, a white shirt with a bib front, a fancy embroidered vest, and a printed silk neckerchief or maybe a string tie with a silver-and-turquoise metal knot. This again showed a Mexican influence. It's extremely rare to see cowboys wearing any kind of jewelry: rings, chains, or earrings would have been simply too dangerous because they'd catch on things. Vanity was satisfied by wearing ornate belts of tooled Spanish leather with Mexican-silver buckles.

A WOMAN'S PLACE

Cowboys lived and worked in an almost exclusively male environment. As countless movies have shown, a woman in a trail camp usually spelled trouble. A few wives of ranchers could ride, rope, and herd cattle as well as a man, but any women involved in outdoor work would have worn men's clothing. The image of the "cowgirl" in buckskin skirts and fringe belongs in Buffalo Bill's Wild West Show.

THE END OF THE DREAM

By the later 1880s, the railroads had reached the southern cattle grounds and there was no need to drive cattle. Ranchers were building more permanent houses and beginning to fence their land with barbed wire. The era of the cowboy was over. However, within 50 years it was being lived all over again on stage and screen. The hit musical *Oklahoma!*

Above: Matriarch Victoria Barkley (Barbara Stanwyck) and her sons in *The Big Valley*, a TV series which ran for four years in the 1960s. Despite an improbably modern hairstyle, Stanwyck's portrayal of a strong, capable widow taking over the running of a ranch set new standards for the depiction of women in westerns.

focuses on the rivalry between cowboys and farmers, summed up in the song "The Farmer and the Cowman." Not surprisingly, the freedom-loving, range-riding cowboy Curly gets the girl in the end.

SINGING COWBOYS

Cowboys were supposed to have sung to restive cattle to calm them down. Taking a cue from this, the early westerns of the 1930s combined action with catchy country and western tunes and spawned a whole procession of showily dressed performers whose thrilling adventures concluded with a song. When John Wayne played Singin' Sandy Saunders in *Riders of Destiny* in 1933, his voice was dubbed, but when Gene Autry, who could sing, stepped in, he was billed as "the Singing Cowboy." Roy Rogers, his great rival, retaliated with "King of the Cowboys." Tex Ritter had been singing cowboy songs on the radio for many years when he appeared in

Below: To many, Roy Rogers was the all-American hero of the 1950s. While he cornered the market in fringed shirts, Trigger the palomino scored top marks with his silver accessories.

Above: A scene from the 1943 musical *Hello Frisco, Hello*. The clothing adopted by that generation of singing cowboys was more suited to the music hall than the open range.

Green Grow the Lilacs, the 1931 play by Lynn Riggs that was the basis for *Oklahoma!* There was even an African-American singing cowboy—Herb Jeffries—in *Harlem on the Prairie* (1937).

THE REAL THING

The earliest cowboy stars had real credentials. Tom Mix, probably the first and most famous screen cowboy, who made 336 films between 1910 and 1935, had worked on a local ranch in Pennsylvania and won awards for rodeo riding. Buck Jones had served in the U.S. Cavalry before becoming a cowboy on a ranch in Oklahoma and then worked in Wild West shows until he joined Universal as a stuntman and backup to Tom Mix. Ken Maynard performed in rodeos before starting his movie career in 1923, doing stunt work. Wearing his trademark white cowboy hat and fancy shirt, he also sang in many of his 90-plus films. Their films were short on realism, big on stunt riding and fancy costumes (oddly, given their backgrounds, none of these cowboy stars objected to the entirely un-authentic outfits they had to wear). If you're costuming a singing cowboy, forget everything this text has to say about accuracy: get an outsize white hat and a lot of fringe and grab a guitar.

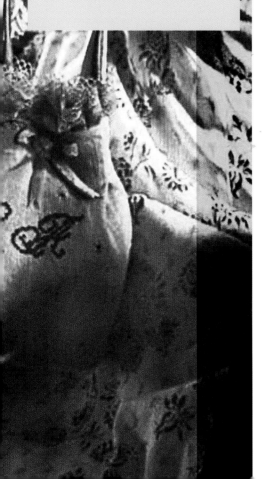

CHAPTER 7

Townsfolk

HAVE IT DELIVERED

The appearance of Sears, Roebuck catalogs in 1872 changed the lives of western women, enabling them to order clothes and equipment by mail. Even if they couldn't afford to buy the clothes themselves, they could keep abreast of fashions and have clothes made up at home. With transportation becoming easier, wealthier townsfolk could now have expensive fabrics imported. Although day dresses were still usually made of cotton or wool, lighter fabrics for evening wear became more common.

SOCIAL CENTERS

By the 1880s, life was settling down and people were moving into real towns. Most were either "cow towns" that had grown up around the railhead or mining towns that had sprung up overnight on the discovery of a new vein. Some were fairly wild places, especially on a Saturday night, when cowboys straight off a drive were out spending their pay. However, as towns expanded, they attracted more "respectable" folk, most of whom settled on the outskirts, put up a white picket fence, and just went on with their lives. Clothing now became an indication of someone's social—and moral—status, especially for women. This can be a minefield for costumers.

Below: Johnny Guitar (1954) starred not one but two feisty, gun-toting women. Joan Crawford, as tough saloon owner Vienna, wore her red bandana in a style that owed more to 1950s fashion than the old West!

SALOON GIRLS

The saloon was the most important place in town. Movies show heavily made-up girls in short skirts and fishnet stockings, garters, and lace-up ankle-length boots. Illustrations, however, suggest this style of dress was highly unlikely. It's almost certainly a kind of can-can costume worn by a very few dancing girls in the revue-style performances put on in the bigger saloon theaters. However, it's true that the women who ran saloons, restaurants, and hotels—and the girls they employed—wore fancy clothes that immediately distinguished them from "respectable" women.

The saloon owner was likely to be a mature woman of some means, dressed in the style of the period. Her clothes were imported from back east or from Europe. This meant long skirts, long sleeves, a nipped-in waist and fitted bodice with perhaps a décolletage, and rich fabrics—taffeta, moiré silk, brocade. Velvet on the whole was reserved for outdoor wear—riding habits and so on. Exact styles need careful research, but the best advice is that—as with the "cowgirl outfits"— almost everything advertised by costume stores is wrong. Avoid anything short, in stretch fabric, or in pastel colors. The ankle boots are fairly authentic and are easily available today but would be only just visible under a long skirt.

Lace mitts, which left the fingers free, were popular accessories, as were fancy gathered purses on a string with ribbon or lace decoration. Silk stockings came in various colors although black was, and is, always safe. Black dresses, however, were rarely worn other than for funerals; solid colors such as wine, deep blue, and dark green were popular.

Above: Most saloon girls wore glamorous outfits from back east, as Faye Dunaway shows in *Little Big Man* (1970). Silk, velvet, and lots of lace were the order of the day—and note the jet choker around her neck.

BEHIND THE PICKET FENCE

Generally, clothing was thought to indicate both a woman's moral virtue and her husband's wealth and status. Young, unmarried girls had a reputation to keep up. High-necked blouses, pastel colors, and a few frills and flounces projected an image of femininity and innocence. Gingham was also popular, as proved over and over by Doris Day. Girls were allowed to wear their hair down to the age of about fifteen.

Right: Professional women were rare in frontier towns in the 1860s, as Jane Seymour discovered weekly in TV's *Dr. Quinn: Medicine Woman*. Her choice of neat, tailored jackets and skirts gave her a respectable image in a man's world, although she was often seen with sleeves rolled up, dealing with birth and death.

HOME STITCHED

Isaac Merrit Singer, from a German immigrant family, marketed his first sewing machine in 1850, improving on an earlier invention by Elias Howe. A clever marketing campaign allowed buyers to pay by installment. This not only revolutionized the professional garment-making industry and brought the price of ready-mades down but also allowed women at home to make their family's clothes far more quickly. This gave women the luxury of adding decorative flounces and frills to even quite ordinary dresses in no time.

or vice versa), with a high neck and leg-of-mutton sleeves. A discreet brooch, perhaps a cameo, might fasten the collar, but as a single, unmarried woman, she could not be seen wearing much personal adornment. Hair was worn with a center part, drawn back in a braid.

HAIR AND MAKEUP

Hairstyles between the 1840s and 1860s did not change much. Generally, hair was pulled back into a bun or braid with a center part. Young girls dressing up might wear their hair in long ringlets at the back instead of a bun. Bangs did not appear until the late 1870s. Also around that time, styles became more elaborate, with hair piled on top of the head and frizzed. Sometimes this was achieved with the aid of hairpieces. Remember, too, that older women often kept on wearing the styles of their youth rather than embracing fashion. Only young girls wore their hair down: on anyone older, it was considered immodest. However, the famous Annie Oakley wore hers down when performing to accentuate her female status.

On the whole, decent women did not wear makeup. Settlers couldn't obtain it anyway, although they probably improvised with candle soot for eye shadow and plant juices for lip coloring. However, those in the entertainment industry wore rouge, dyed their hair, and maybe even tried out the latest in mascara—dabs of melted black wax placed on each lash. A clear, fair complexion was greatly prized: sunburn meant that you did manual work outdoors. Today's cosmetics should be used with care: nothing shimmery or with too much color. Coral and basic red lipstick are fine, but use them sparingly.

Above: A scene from Sergio Leone's *C'era una volta il West* (*Once Upon a Time in the West*) shows a cross-section of townsfolk. It's a good reference for costuming different generations and types of character.

JEWELRY

Few women wore much jewelry until they were married. Accepting jewelry or even clothing from a man you weren't related to was morally dubious. Brooches, a locket on a gold chain, and small earrings—definitely no gold hoops—were about as far as one went. Absolutely to be avoided when costuming are any items of "western-themed" jewelry advertised today: earrings or cuff links in the shape of spurs or six-guns, charm bracelets, and so on.

THE GENERAL STORE

The General Store sold dry goods, clothing, hardware, tools, guns and ammunition, and whatever luxuries might have arrived. It was the complete one-stop shopping experience. Stores also sold fabric off the roll by the yard, and these transactions were normally handled by the woman of the store: men were not expected to know about such things. The store was usually

STYLE TIP

Dresses of this period involve some complex tailoring and are not easy to make. For serious re-enactment, you might prefer to splurge on buying a dress and then make your own accessories. However, there are several Web sites offering patterns for a basic dress or skirt and blouse. Shawls are easy to make, bonnets less so, but again, there are patterns available online.

a family operation, so behind the counter you might find the storekeeper, his wife, and maybe a grown-up son or daughter pressed into service. He would be wearing a standard men's outfit or maybe bib overalls and might have sleeve protectors pulled over his forearms. She would be wearing a cotton skirt and blouse, rather than a dress, and an apron: neat and clean but not fancy and probably in subdued colors. She'd have her long hair in a bun. Their customers would be local farmers and their wives, dressed similarly. Farmers might wear bib overalls for general work, but there's no indication that cowboys or ranch hands wore these.

GAMBLERS AND DANDIES

Gambling flourished, especially in New Orleans and the towns along the Mississippi River. Most saloons had a gaming room at the back. Traveling gamblers worked the tables, separating workers from their wages until they were driven out of town by public opinion. Then they took to the

Below: Ava Gardner played Lillie Langtry—"the Jersey Lily"—in *The Life and Times of Judge Roy Bean*. The notorious "hanging judge" named his town, and the saloon in which he held court, after the British actress who was famous for her elegant outfits.

riverboats, where, between 1840 and 1860, they were a regular and somewhat glamorous sight. The TV series *Maverick* (1957–62) featured the adventures of the Maverick brothers, city slickers slightly ill at ease in the unruly West but generally one step ahead of the game. They were always elegantly dressed in city clothes: frock coat, white frilled shirt, brocade vest, tight light-colored pants without cuffs, short boots, and a string tie or a cravat fastened with a mother-of-pearl pin. An ivory-handled cane is a good accessory here.

SUPPORTING CAST

Other characters in an average town might include the telegraph operator, usually a man although women were so employed, too. He'd be recognizable from the elbow-length cotton sleeve protectors worn over his white shirt and would be wearing a vest: this was a responsible and respectable job. The blacksmith, an essential character, would be wearing a leather apron. The sheriff and his deputies, crucial to the safe running of the town, spent their time in the sheriff's office, which usually contained a few jail cells.

THE CHURCH

Church services were usually held in the saloon until the congregation outgrew it and a proper church could be built. Religion was very much a "come as you are" affair: the preacher might wear a black frock coat to distinguish him, but there was nothing in the way of liturgical garments. Most folk had a Sunday-best outfit and wore a hat to the service.

Below: Bart and Bret Maverick, the best-dressed gamblers in town, played by Jack Kelly and James Garner.

CHAPTER 8

Outlaws, Lawmen, and Gunslingers

FINGER ON THE PULSE

The Assassination of Jesse James by the Coward Robert Ford was scrupulously researched. Not only do costumes compare well with photographs of James as a snappy dresser but apparently the top half of Brad Pitt's left middle finger was erased by computer graphics in every close-up to conform to the real James's disfigurement. Re-enactment, of course, needn't go that far. Legend also has it that Brad Pitt threatened to pull out of the movie if anyone tried to change the title.

The chaotic state of the country and the lingering resentment after the Civil War combined to produce a number of generally lawless characters. Many of these, such as Jesse James, were elevated to the status of hero by the newly emerging dime novels, which chronicled their exploits as freedom fighters and conveniently overlooked their ruthlessness. Already legends in their own lifetimes, they have gone on to appear in countless movies and TV shows. Along with the rise of the outlaw went the rise of the lawman, a fearless individual who rode the land righting wrongs and defending the innocent. Well, according to the movies, anyway.

Hollywood has been just as culpable as the dime novels in romanticizing these real characters. Sergio Leone's *Once Upon a Time in the West*, for example, treated its characters as heroic figures. Sam Peckinpah's movie *The Wild Bunch* was one of the first to show characters as scruffy, trail-stained, and generally more true to life, but even before that, a few production designers took the trouble to research costumes properly.

Above: Henry Fonda played a suave Wyatt Earp in *My Darling Clementine* (1946). The front-laced bodice, flounced skirt and peasant blouse worn by saloon girl Linda Darnell show a Mexican influence just right for a character named Chihuahua.

OUTLAWS

The first thing to establish is that these aren't cowboys; they're ordinary townsfolk on the wrong side of the law. They may be on horseback, but they dress in dark wool pants and coats, vests, white shirts, and sometimes ties. Derby hats are much in evidence. There's a kind of formality to their dress, as if they were living up to their wanted posters. An exception might be that in the months

immediately after the Civil War, some—the remnants of Quantrill's famous Raiders, for example—were still wearing items of the Confederate uniform: a gray army shirt, for example, or a kepi-style cap.

GUNMEN

The term gunslinger (itself thought to be a movie invention) applies to anyone, hero or villain, who earns his living by his skill with a gun. The archetypal gunslinger is a loner, often dressed in black, with a low-slung gun belt and holster tied down on his thigh so he can draw more cleanly.

In movies, the market in gunslingers was cornered by Jack Palance, but TV's most celebrated 1950s' gunfighter was Paladin, hero of *Have Gun— Will Travel*, played elegantly by Richard Boone. He dressed entirely in black, the only ornament being the silver image of a chess-piece knight on his holster that advertised his status as knight errant, a righter of wrongs, for hire.

It's a great image for costuming, even if the low-cut holster, which allowed a fast draw, is an anachronism. But avoid tricks such as twirling the gun with a finger through the trigger guard. They're almost certainly inventions of the movies: in reality, they were far too dangerous to be indulged in by men whose lives depended on their weapons.

JESSE JAMES

Jesse James, along with his brother, Frank, was portrayed as a Robin Hood figure, robbing from rich Northern corporations and giving to the poor of the defeated Confederacy. Even today, many towns hold annual re-enactments of the James brothers' various bank robberies and train

Above: The black-garbed gang in *The Quick and the Dead* (1995) look suitably sinister, despite the fact that Gene Hackman (center) is wearing a neat derby and a city-style suit.

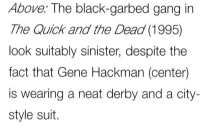

STYLE TIP

Cowboys grew facial hair as protection against chapped lips and because shaving on the range was difficult. For townsfolk, it conferred a kind of status. The horseshoe mustache, which continued down each side of the mouth and resembled an upside-down horseshoe, was a popular style. For a quick change, stick-on mustaches can be bought from any costume store.

Above: In *The Assassination of Jesse James by the Coward Robert Ford*, Brad Pitt followed the real outlaw's dress style in every detail.

holdups. Jesse James is one of the most recognizable "characters" you could choose to portray, although there's a small snag: since he died at age 34, this is a character for young men. Jesse has featured in at least 20 movies, played by Tyrone Power, Audie Murphy, Robert Wagner, Robert Duvall, Kris Kristofferson, and, most recently, Brad Pitt in the 2007 movie *The Assassination of Jesse James by the Coward Robert Ford.*

BILLY THE KID

The opposite of a snappy dresser, William Bonney—Billy the Kid—is shown in photos wearing a loose, dark shirt with a vest, baggy pants tucked into ankle boots, and a large bandana. He wears a battered high-crowned broad-brimmed hat with a scarf tied around it. His nemesis, Sheriff Pat Garrett, couldn't be more different. Photographs show him in a tight suit, winged collar, and studded tie. Gunned down by Garrett at the age of 21, the Kid is a bit of a mystery and little is known about his life, but this hasn't deterred movie directors. In 1930, King Vidor made *Billy the Kid*, starring Johnny Mack Brown. Arthur Penn's *The Left-Handed Gun* (1958), starring Paul Newman, was famed for its authenticity, but was later outshone by Sam Peckinpah's *Pat Garrett and Billy the Kid*, starring Kris Kristofferson, in 1973. But not even Emilio Estevez, who played Billy in *Young Guns* (1988), was really young enough to be convincing as the teenage Kid.

BELLE STARR

Belle Starr acquired the reputation of a "bandit queen," leading a band of horse and cattle thieves in Oklahoma's Indian Territory. She had several husbands (some simultaneously) and left her various children with her mother while away on adventures. She mixed with all the outlaws of the day, including Jesse James and the Younger brothers, part of the James gang, and in 1883 became the first female ever tried for a major crime by the celebrated "Hanging Judge" Parker in Arkansas. She is also said to have read widely and played piano, so perhaps it's not surprising that one photo shows her sitting sidesaddle with a cockade hat and elegant black velvet riding habit and another shows her in a fine velvet dress with frills at the cuffs—but with a six-gun in her hand and another stuffed into her waistband. Although these are no doubt "publicity" shots, in all her exploits she doesn't appear to have adopted men's dress. So if you're dressing Belle Starr, no pants, please.

LAWMEN

What's the difference between a sheriff and a U.S. marshal? A sheriff had responsibility for a town and its immediate area and was elected by the townspeople, whereas the office of marshal was a government appointment and carried responsibility for a federal judicial district. Both had the power to swear in deputies from among the citizens when they needed backup. Neither wore a uniform: the tin star said it all. A marshal, however, would dress more formally: a frock coat, white shirt and vest, and wool pants, for example, whereas sheriffs are usually shown wearing standard work pants, shirt, and vest, but with plain shirts rather than anything fancy out of respect for the office. This is exemplified by Gary Cooper's character Will Kane in *High Noon*. About to retire and settle down with his new bride,

---

Right: This remarkable photograph of Belle Starr shows her as a bizarre and contradictory—but hardly feminine—figure.

BELLE STARR

" *Belle Starr, Belle Starr, tell me where you have gone Since old Oklahoma's sandhills you did roam? Is it Heaven's wide streets that you're tying your reins Or single-footing somewhere below?*

Eight lovers they say combed your waving black hair, Eight men knew the feel of your dark velvet waist, Eight men heard the sounds of your tan leather skirt, Eight men heard the bark of the guns that you wore. "

Woody Guthrie, *Ballad of Belle Starr* (1947)

he has to confront one last enemy in gunslinger Frank Miller, arriving in town to settle an old score. The "ordinary guy" dignity and moral strength of Cooper's character made him an archetype of frontier manhood, "doing what a man's got to do."

WYATT EARP

Probably the most famous real-life U.S. marshal, Wyatt Earp lived to the remarkable age of 80 in spite of his exploits at the O.K. Corral and cleaning up the town of Tombstone. Photographs of Wyatt in his heyday show him in a high-buttoned suit and derby hat, only a little less the dandy than his friend Masterson. Both the 1950s' TV series *The Life and Legend of Wyatt Earp*, which starred Hugh O'Brian in a number of brocade vests and an oddly flat-brimmed hat, and Kevin Costner's 1994 movie portrayal, less glossy in a black frock coat, caught the essence of the character. Earp's real distinguishing feature was the gun he carried—a long-barreled six-gun known as the Buntline Special. He reputedly used it to pistol-whip opponents, thus disarming them without shooting.

Below: Ten years after *My Darling Clementine*, the Wyatt Earp–Doc Holliday story was remade as *Gunfight at the O.K. Corral*. Burt Lancaster (Earp) and Kirk Douglas (Holliday) followed tradition in being elegantly turned out.

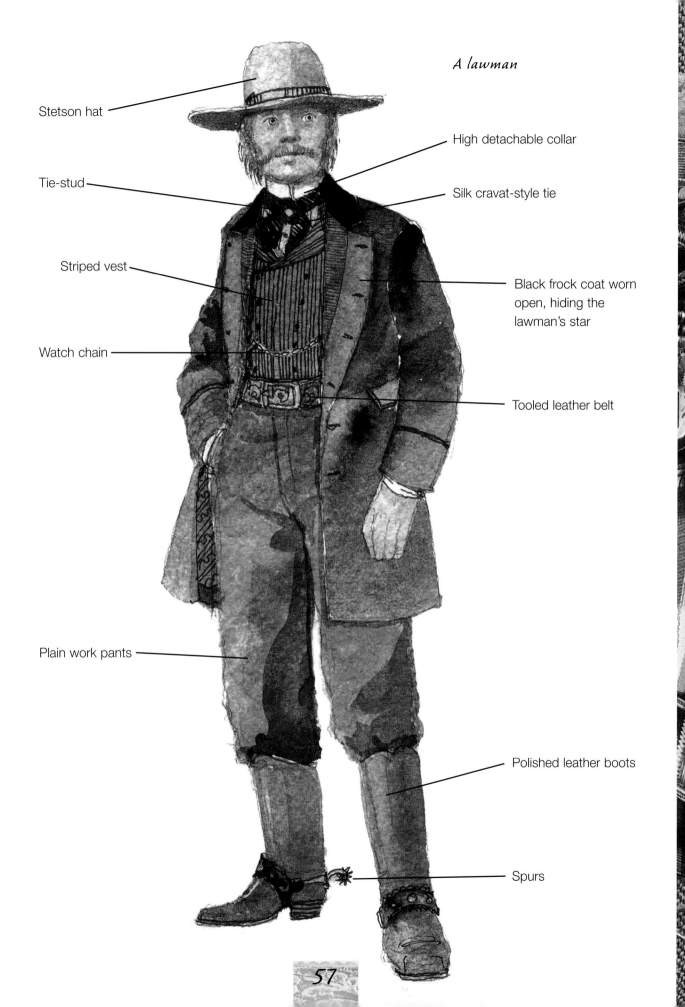

A lawman

Stetson hat

High detachable collar

Tie-stud

Silk cravat-style tie

Striped vest

Black frock coat worn open, hiding the lawman's star

Watch chain

Tooled leather belt

Plain work pants

Polished leather boots

Spurs

MUSICAL LEGENDS

Musicals such as Irving Berlin's *Annie Get Your Gun* and *Calamity Jane* include pretty much all the typical characters of the Wild West: the sharp-shooting tomboy, the handsome cowboy hero, the "real" Buffalo Bill, and Chief Sitting Bull, hero of the Lakota Sioux. If you're costuming a production like this, do you go for authenticity and check out the original or, as advocated in *The Man Who Shot Liberty Valance*, "print the legend"? Most productions have gone for the latter.

CALAMITY JANE

The real Calamity, or Martha Jane Canary, was a hard-drinking Native American fighter, mule driver, and scout, who dressed like a man in order to do a man's job. She was also a part-time actress, but the few photos of her in women's clothing show nothing more exotic than a rather severe dark wool skirt and blouse and a cowboy hat. The version of her dreamed up in the 1953 film *Calamity Jane* has Doris Day entirely and endearingly feminine underneath her tight buckskins and with short, bubbly curls. In *The Paleface* (1948), Calamity was portrayed by Jane Russell, queen of the parody western, whose curvy figure was, as usual, shown off to good effect.

BUFFALO BILL

In addition to being a soldier, scout, Native American fighter, and buffalo hunter, William Frederick Cody was, above all, a showman. In 1883, he put together Buffalo Bill's Wild West, attracting several real western personalities to take

Left: Doris Day's girl-next-door image managed to make even the hard-riding, hard-drinking Calamity Jane into an attractive tomboy—but in reality, women rarely wore men's clothes.

part. The show included a Pony Express ride, Native Americans attacking a wagon train, and a stagecoach holdup before ending with a re-enactment of Custer's Last Stand, with Bill himself as General Custer. The show toured England and Europe to huge acclaim before setting up just outside the 1893 Chicago World's Fair and stealing many of its visitors. Bill himself was so flamboyant in appearance that it would be difficult to over-costume him.

ANNIE OAKLEY

She was hardly a westerner but an excellent shot and a good performer: joining Buffalo Bill's Wild West Show in 1889, she was billed as "Little Miss Sure Shot." Posters show her dressed in a tight, fitted, frilled bodice and pleated calf-length skirt and wearing her long hair loose under a cowboy hat. Costumes in the fictional versions of her life, however, were less restrained. Ethel Merman, in the original 1946 Broadway musical *Annie Get Your Gun*, wore a fringed skirt and bolero tie. Betty Hutton, in the 1950 film version, wore a rhinestone-encrusted costume of shirt, skirt, ankle boots, and cowboy hat that would have surprised the original, while Howard Keel, as husband Frank Butler, wore cow skin. Other Annies were Barbara Stanwyck in the 1935 film *Annie Oakley* and Geraldine Chaplin in *Buffalo Bill and the Indians* (1976).

Right: The real Annie Oakley wore a modest outfit that emphasized her hour-glass figure. Buffalo Bill played up her femininity because it was unusual at the time for a woman to be such a good shot.

BUFFALO BILL'S WILD WEST.
CONGRESS, ROUGH RIDERS OF THE WORLD.

MISS ANNIE OAKLEY,
THE PEERLESS LADY WING-SHOT.

Glossary

bandana A silk or cotton scarf or neckerchief.

bayeta Brownish-red fine wool fabric.

block-printing Making a pattern on fabric by stamping images carved on a wood block.

bowie knife A hunting knife with a curved tip and a guard for the hand.

broadcloth Closely woven fabric of wool, cotton, or worsted with a lustrous finish, so called because it was woven on a wide loom.

brocade Any rich, stiff silk fabric with a pattern woven into it.

brogans Lace-up shoes that reach to the ankle, like desert boots.

buckskin The tanned hide of deer, elk, or antelope.

can-can A dance originating in French music halls.

canvas Coarse cloth made of hemp or linen.

capote A wool coat made from blanket cloth.

chaps Coverings for the legs that tied over the pants.

chilkat Fabric with traditional designs woven from goat hair and cedar bark.

cravat A scarf worn instead of a tie.

derby A round-crowned hat with a curved brim; known as a bowler in Europe.

dime novels Cheap books of sensational stories.

epaulettes Ornamental shoulder pieces on a military uniform.

flannel A soft, light wool fabric with a slight nap.

flax A blue-flowered plant whose fibrous stems are made into cloth.

gingham Woven, checked cotton fabric.

Henley style Having three buttons at the neck.

hussar jacket An elegant double-breasted jacket decorated with braiding and frog fastenings. A frog is a fastening of looped braid or cord, commonly used in nineteenth-century military uniforms.

jerk Strips of dried meat.

kepi A round military cap with a flat top and a visor.

lapped Wrapped or folded.

linsey-woolsey A fabric made of wool mixed with cotton or linen.

medicine bag A bag for holding ritual items such as bones, hair, and sacred stones.

militia A military group raised from the general population (as opposed to a regular, conscripted army).

moonshine Home-brewed whiskey.

paisley A pattern based on leaf shapes or a soft wool fabric printed with this pattern.

pinto A black-and-white or brown-and-white horse; from the Spanish for "painted."

rawhide Hide that has not been tanned.

sombrero A high-crowned, wide-brimmed hat, from the Spanish for "shade."

stovepipe A straight, narrow shape, used to describe pants, hats, and boots.

tepee A conical tent made of animal hide stretched over a pole structure.

vaquero A Mexican cowboy.

velvet A thick-piled fabric made of silk or cotton.

wampum Beads made from seashells.

wearing blanket A blanket intended to be worn like a shawl, not just for sleeping.

wrangler A cowboy who takes care of the spare horses on a cattle drive.

Further Information

BOOKS

Brown, Dee. *The American West.* Touchstone, 1995.

Chan, Sucheng, Douglas Henry Daniels, Mario Garcia, and Terry Wilson. *Peoples of Color in the American West.* Houghton Mifflin, 1993.

Draper, Allison Stark. *What People Wore During the Westward Expansion: Clothing, Costumes, and Uniforms Throughout American History.* PowerKids Press, 2001.

Hine, Robert, and John Mack Faragher. *Frontiers: A Short History of the American West.* Yale University Press, 2008.

Hirschfelder, Arlene. *Native Americans.* Dorling Kindersley, 2000.

Hunt, Ben W. *The Complete Book of Indian Crafts and Lore.* Goldencraft, 1974.

Lackmann, Ronald W. *Women of the Western Frontier in Fact, Fiction and Film.* McFarland, 1997.

La Crosse, Richard. *The Frontier Rifleman.* Union City, Tenn.: Pioneer Press, 1989.

Rollins, Peter C., and O'Connor, John E. *Hollywood's West, in Film, Television and History.* Lexington: University Press of Kentucky, 2005.

Sinclair, Clive. *True Tales of the Wild West.* Picador, 2007.

Tunis, Edward. *Pioneer Living: An Illustrated Guide to Pioneer Life in America.* Globe Pequot Press, 2000.

WEB SITES

http://cowboyoutfitters.com/index.html
This Web site supplies western clothes and accessories for you and your horse.

www.legendsofamerica.com
History, photos, and information on all aspects of the West, including places to visit.

www.maskharat.org/2003/costumes.htm
San Francisco-based site with links to other sites, including history of costume, retailers, and pattern libraries.

http://mman.home.att.net
"Malachite's Big Hole": information on mountain men and fur traders, plus links to firsthand accounts of life in the mountains and trapping.

www.nationalcowboymuseum.org
Web site of the museum that houses a turn-of-the-century town and interactive history galleries focusing on the American cowboy, rodeos, Native American culture, and other American West subjects.

www.native-languages.org
Information on Native American cultures, including maps.

www.sewingcentral.com
Has patterns for sale and illustrations of clothing; covers frontier and Native American clothing.

www.thecowboycloset.com
Commercial suppliers of traditional clothing but useful for visual references.

www.varsityrendezvous.com/pdf/clothing.pdf
Information on mountain men clothing, with patterns.

Source List

A selection of movies and TV series with American West themes.

MOVIES

Historical

The Alamo (1960), dir. John Wayne, with John Wayne, Richard Widmark

The Alamo (2004), dir. John Lee Hancock, with Dennis Quaid, Billy Bob Thornton

The Mountain Men (1980), dir. Richard Lang, with Charlton Heston, Brian Keith

Once Upon a Time in the West (1968), dir. Sergio Leone, with Claudia Cardinale and Henry Fonda

The Texas Rangers (2001), dir Steve Miner, with James Van Der Beek, Usher Raymond

Cavalry

Fort Apache (1948), dir. John Ford, with Henry Fonda, John Wayne

Rio Grande (1951), dir. John Ford, with John Wayne, Maureen O'Hara

She Wore a Yellow Ribbon (1949), dir. John Ford, with John Wayne, Joanne Dru

Outlaws

The Assassination of Jesse James by the Coward Robert Ford (2007), dir. Andrew Dominik, with Brad Pitt, Casey Affleck

Butch Cassidy and the Sundance Kid (1969), dir. George Roy Hill, with Paul Newman, Robert Redford

Gunfight at the OK Corral (1957), dir. John Sturges, with Burt Lancaster, Kirk Douglas

High Noon (1952), dir. Fred Zinnemann, with Gary Cooper, Grace Kelly

The Life and Times of Judge Roy Bean (1972), dir. John Huston, with Paul Newman, Ava Gardner

The Magnificent Seven (1960), dir. John Sturges, with Yul Brynner, Steve McQueen

The 'Man With No Name' trilogy: *A Fistful of Dollars* (1964)/*For a Few Dollars More* (1965)/*The Good, the Bad and the Ugly* (1966), all dir. Sergio Leone, with Clint Eastwood

My Darling Clementine (1946), dir. John Ford, with Henry Fonda, Victor Mature

Pat Garrett and Billy the Kid (1973), dir. Sam Peckinpah, with Kris Kristofferson, James Coburn

Shane (1953), dir. George Stevens, with Alan Ladd, Jean Arthur

The Wild Bunch (1969), dir. Sam Peckinpah, with William Holden, Ernest Borgnine

Native Americans

Cheyenne Autumn (1964), dir. John Ford, with Richard Widmark, Carroll Baker

The Comancheros (1961), dir. Michael Curtiz, with John Wayne, Stuart Whitman

Dances With Wolves (1990), dir. Kevin Costner, with Kevin Costner, Mary McDonnell

The Last Wagon (1956), dir. Delmer Daves, with Richard Widmark, Felicia Farr

Little Big Man (1970), dir. Arthur Penn with Dustin Hoffman, Faye Dunaway

A Man Called Horse (1970), dir. Elliot Silverstein, with Richard Harris, Judith Anderson

The Searchers (1956), dir. John Ford, with John Wayne, Natalie Wood

Other classic westerns

The Big Country (1958), dir. William Wyler, with Gregory Peck, Jean Simmons

How the West Was Won (1963), dir. Henry Hathaway, John Ford, George Marshall, with Debbie Reynolds, Henry Fonda

The Man Who Shot Liberty Valance (1962), dir. John Ford, with James Stewart, John Wayne

Stagecoach (1939), dir. John Ford, with Claire Trevor, John Wayne

Musicals

Annie Get your Gun (1950), dir. George Sidney, with Betty Hutton, Howard Keel

Calamity Jane (1953), dir. David Butler, with Doris Day, Howard Keel

Oklahoma! (1955), dir. Fred Zinnemann, with Shirley Jones, Gordon MacRae

Seven Brides for Seven Brothers (1954), dir. Stanley Donan, with Jane Powell, Howard Keel

Off-beat westerns

Blazing Saddles (1974), dir. Mel Brooks, with Gene Wilder, Cleavon Little

Brokeback Mountain (2006), dir. Ang Lee, with Heath Ledger, Jake Gyllenhaal

Johnny Guitar (1954), dir. Nicholas Ray, with Joan Crawford, Sterling Hayden

The Misfits (1961), dir. John Huston, with Marilyn Monroe, Clark Gable

The Paleface (1948), dir. Norman Z. McLeod, with Bob Hope, Jane Russell

The Quick and the Dead (1995), dir. Sam Raimi, with Gene Hackman, Sharon Stone

TV

The Adventures of Jim Bowie (1956–8), with Scott Forbes

The Adventures of Rin Tin Tin (1954–9), with Lee Aaker, James Brown

Annie Oakley (1954–7), with Gail Davis, Brad Johnson

Bat Masterson (1958–61), with Gene Barry

The Big Valley (1965–9), with Barbara Stanwyck

Bonanza (1959–73), with Lorne Greene, Michael Landon

Bronco (1958–62), with Ty Hardin

Bury My Heart at Wounded Knee (2007), with Aidan Quinn, August Schellenberg

Cheyenne (1955–62), with Clint Walker

The Cisco Kid (1951–4), with Duncan Renaldo, Leo Carillo

Daniel Boone (1964–7), with Fess Parker

Dr. Quinn, Medicine Woman (1993–8), with Jane Seymour

Gunsmoke (1955–75), with James Arness, Dennis Weaver

Have Gun Will Travel (1957–63), with Richard Boone

The High Chaparral (1967–71), with Leif Erickson, Linda Cristal

Laramie (1959–63), with Robert Fuller and John Smith

Lawman (1958–62), with John Russell, Peter Brown

The Life and Legend of Wyatt Earp (1955–7), with Hugh O'Brian

The Little House on the Prairie (1974–84), with Michael Landon and Melissa Gilbert

The Lone Ranger (1949–57), with Clayton Moore, Jay Silverheels

Maverick (1957–62), with James Garner, Jack Kelly

Rawhide (1959–65), with Clint Eastwood

The Roy Rogers Show (1951–7), with Roy Rogers, Dale Evans, Trigger the horse and Bullet the dog

Sugarfoot (1957–61), with Will Hutchins

The Virginian (1962–71), with James Drury, Doug McClure

Wagon Train (1957–65), with Ward Bond, Robert Fuller

The Young Riders (1989–92), with Stephen Baldwin, Josh Brolin

Index

Numbers in **bold** refer to illustrations.